I0455350

Improve Your Writing from A to Z

2009 Edition

By Ross Edwards

This page intentionally left blank.

Improve Your Writing from A to Z, 2009 Edition
©2008-2009 by Ross Edwards, author and editor.

First printing, January 2009, 0 9 8 7 6 5 4 3 2 1

Printed by CreateSpace™ under agreement with Exuberance Press,
Chandler, Arizona, USA

ISBN-10: 14414 0032X
ISBN-13: 9781441400321

All Rights Reserved. No part of this book may be reproduced
without written permission from the author or publisher, except for
brief quotations in articles and reviews. For information please
email the author at: rossedwardsbooks@gmail.com

Acknowledgments: While I cannot possibly thank everybody in the
space I have here, I am grateful to the following contributors
whose assistance to this project, direct or indirect, made a
difference for the better: Tom and Mary Zemites, Mark Gula, Ray
Rogissart, Ruthann Smejkal, Eddie and Joanne Bahr, and my wife
Stephanie and daughter Alexandra.

This book is for information and entertainment purposes only.
This book does not make any guarantee, promise, or assurance as
to the factual accuracy of any information contained herein. All
information in this book has been compiled from sources
determined by the author to be reliable, and the author has made
efforts to eliminate errors and questionable data. Nevertheless, the
possibility of error, in a work of this nature, always exists. The
author, publisher, and other pertinent parties are not responsible for
losses or consequences that may occur due to use of the
information in this book. Readers who believe they have
discovered an error are encouraged to write and inform us, so that
the errors, if verified, can be corrected in a subsequent edition or
editions. This book is not intended to provide legal advice. The
information in this book may not be suitable for all consumer
situations. For legal advice, consult an attorney licensed in your
jurisdiction. This book is produced independently and is not

endorsed, sponsored, or approved by any publisher of any other writing style guide, periodical, textbook, or reference work.

Bulk purchasing arrangements are available for educational, commercial, and governmental institutions. Contact the vendor from which you acquired this book or the author for further information.

Foreword

Congratulations! By acquiring this book, you have taken a step toward refining and polishing your writing skills to a higher degree of professionalism and precision. As author, I extend my best wishes to you and hope this book serves you well, whether you are a college student seeking to improve your grades, a career-hunter seeking an excellent job, or a career-climber taking another step up the ladder.

It is not necessary for you to read this book from cover to cover as you would read a novel or how-to guide. This is a reference work, and all entries are alphabetized to make the book easy to use. Keep this book by your side while you write and simply look up the information you need. Not sure whether to use an apostrophe? Look up *apostrophes* under *A*. Not sure whether to write *infer* or *imply*? Look up *infer, imply* under *I*. Not sure whether you can use parentheses in a phrase? Look up *parentheses* under *P*. Having difficulty determining whether *who* or *whom* is correct in your sentence? You guessed it: look up *who, whom* under *W*. It really is just that simple.

Despite being simple and straightforward, the writing styles this book teaches are appropriate for use at any level, from casual to professional. I searched many professional style guides to determine the prevailing usage for writing rules and formats. In most respects, there is broad agreement among style guides. APA style, MLA style, Bluebook style, ALWD style, and the rest generally differ only on usage that is peculiar in their given niche.

Where the style guides disagreed, I followed American usage over international usage, prevailing trends over dated styles, and conservative precision over discretionary flavor. Where extremely formal usage differs from common usage, even where common usage is professionally acceptable, the entry will state the difference and offer you both options for your document. For example, see *italics*. The general style rule you read in this book will be correct 99% of the time, and for those times when that remaining 1% might make a big difference, I made a note of it so you could decide for yourself how to proceed. In some cases, disagreement between style guides and regional usage was so extensive that I turned to functional applications to determine which usage would most likely emerge as the long-term best rule. For example, see *time*.

If your work and your writing send you into full-time journalism, legal analysis, or postgraduate academic writing, you will likely be instructed to strictly conform to a particular style guide, such as the *Bluebook* (law), the *APA Style Guide* (medicine, social research), or the *Chicago Manual of Style* (journalism). If your required style guide and this book conflict, by all means follow your required style guide. I certainly do not want you to fail your doctoral dissertation or have your interlocutory pleading rejected by a finicky judge. If you are writing on that level, this book will serve as a quick and easy reference for your day-to-day work, but you will need to adhere to your specific style requirements when it is time to do the heavy lifting.

For the rest of us, however, this book should be correct for virtually all the writing we do. Most people are perfectly capable of writing clear, concise, and understandable documents, but were either taught incorrect rules in grammar school or were forced to guess at proper usage and never had their mistakes corrected. If you are a college student, career-hunter, or career-climber reading this book, you are already in the right frame of mind to break those old bad habits and learn the correct usage and styles in your writing. When we raise the bar to expect a higher level of professionalism in writing, both writer and reader benefit. It is with that principle in mind that I created this book. I hope this book truly does help you Improve Your Writing from A to Z. Good luck!

- Ross Edwards, author and editor

a, an

Use the article *a* before consonant sounds:

A historic concert;
A one-year contract (sounds as if it begins with a *w*);
A united front (sounds like *you*).

Use the article *an* before vowel sounds:

An energetic performance;
An honorable knight (the *h* is silent);
An LCD TV (sounds like it begins with the syllable *el*);
An 18-story building.

abbreviations

The first usage in an entire document of an abbreviation of a proper noun should spell out the source in full, especially if the document uses multiple abbreviations. Typically, the abbreviation follows the source and is placed in parentheses. Do not abbreviate at all if you are only going to be referring to the source once, and consider not abbreviating if you are only going to be referring to the source a small number of times.

Since 1946, Zemites Family Catering Services (ZFCS) has served the Tri-State area. ZFCS is ready to ensure that your dinner event is successful and memorable.

The U.S. Department of Health and Human Services (DHHS) administers the State Children's Health Insurance Program (SCHIP) for all fifty states. Each state receives federal matching funds from DHHS for allocation to the state's SCHIP entitlements.

Vincent was remanded to the custody of the Montana Department of Corrections. (no abbreviation)

Ubiquitous abbreviations can be used without first defining the source in most documents, but the more formal the document, the more likely the source is needed.

Mike Portnoy's DVD collection includes hundreds of titles spanning many genres.

Stephanie performed CPR, but she was unable to resuscitate the victim.

Beware! Abbreviations that seem ubiquitous can sometimes be confusing due to duplication or local usage.

Monty graduated from FSU in 1998. (Florida State University or Fresno State University?)

Rush performed at the TCC Arena in 1978. (At the Tucson Civic Center Arena in Arizona or at the Tarrant County Civic Arena in Ft. Worth, Texas?)

Spell out an abbreviation that begins a sentence. Sometimes, doing so will suffice to define an abbreviation, and you will not need to use parentheses:

Oregon State University's homecoming game is next Saturday. Any OSU students who wish to attend should purchase tickets online no later than Tuesday. (No reader will think that "OSU" means Ohio State University, even though that school also uses the "OSU" abbreviation, because the previous sentence specifically named Oregon.)

For extremely formal usage, such as statutory or regulatory drafting, contract formation, or academic reference, it is preferable that a *Definitions* section contains the source noun or phrase and that the body of the text uses the abbreviation exclusively. If the abbreviation has periods in the text, define with periods. If the abbreviation does not have periods in the text, define without periods. For example, if you use *SEC* in your rules, don't define the term *Securities and Exchange Commission*. Instead define *SEC*. Your definition of *SEC* can and should include language identifying the *Securities and Exchange Commission* -- or the *Southeastern Conference*, as applicable. Use *S.E.C.* (with periods) in the text if you have defined the term as *S.E.C.* (with periods). Use *SEC* (without periods) in the text if you have defined the term as *SEC* (without periods).

abdicate, abrogate

To *abdicate* is to surrender responsibility or authority. To *abrogate* is to wrongfully impede a legal right or the execution of a contract.

Mike Portnoy and John Petrucci are not likely to abdicate control over the creative direction of Dream Theater after their difficulties in 1998.

The Arizona Constitution includes an anti-abrogation clause preventing newly-enacted laws from negating a citizen's right to recover damages in court.

ability, capacity

Ability means the state of being able to do something. *Capacity* means the power of receiving or containing. Avoid using *capacity* in the context of mental capacity, because *mental capacity* is a legal term of art encumbered with additional meaning that *ability* does not connote. The exception, of course, would be if your document actually pertains to the legal concept of mental capacity.

able-bodied

Spelled and hyphenated thus. Be careful with usage if your document may be read by audiences sensitive to disability issues.

about, approximately

About is inexact and suggests a rough estimate. *Approximately* implies accuracy.

We have about five hours left until the deadline. (Definitely more than four and less than six, but it's difficult to say if we will be safe at the four-and-a-half-hour mark.)

We have approximately five hours left until the deadline. (Give or take a few minutes.)

above, over

When indicating quantity, avoid using prepositions that indicate direction or location. See **over, more than**.

aboveground

Spelled thus. Compound words eventually lose hyphenation through usage. James installed an above-ground swimming pool in his yard would have been correct in 1970.

abrogate, abdicate

See **abdicate, abrogate**.

accept, except

Accept means to receive or to agree with something. *Except* means to exclude or reject. These two words, nearly antonyms, are commonly misused. A reply to the hiring manager stating I except the position, taken literally, means that you are rejecting the job offer. In addition to the risk that you will lose the job offer by mistakenly answering the opposite of what you meant, the employer may revoke the job offer upon discovering that you do not know the difference between *accept* and *except*.

accommodate

Spelled thus. Two *c*s, two *m*s, two *o*s, two *a*s.

acknowledgment

Spelled thus. Do not put another *e* after the *g*. That is British English, not American English. The related verb is still *acknowledge* in both forms.

Dream Theater acknowledges Yes as a major influence, but does not include Yes among the acknowledgments in their album liner notes.

action verbs

In general, action verbs are shorter and more direct than passive verbs. Use verbs instead of nouns to add action to your writing.

Wrong: The producer shall ensure that the new album is completed on schedule through:
1. Coordination of the schedules of band members for optimal use of studio time;
2. Selection of a talented engineer for the track recording process; and

3. Cooperation with the label's marketing staff so that promotion begins on time.

Right: The producer shall ensure that the new album is completed on schedule by:
1. Coordinating the scheduling of band members for optimal use of studio time;
2. Selecting a talented engineer for the track recording process; and
3. Cooperating with the label's marketing staff so they can begin promoting the album.

When choosing an action verb, simplest is often best:

Don't write:	Write:
give consideration to	consider
make payment	pay
give recognition to	recognize
maximize	increase
compartmentalize	arrange
utilize	use

active voice

Write in the active voice. Active sentences are usually shorter and more forceful than passive sentences. When you write in the active voice, it becomes easier to improve a document, when appropriate, with strong, precise, or vivid verbs. Active voice identifies an actor. Putting the actor before the verb clarifies who is responsible for an act.

Wrong:
The food was eaten. *By whom?*
The prices were lowered. *By whom?*
The late-night project was started. *By whom?*

Right:
Strong:
Roger ate the food.

The manager lowered the prices.
Kristin started the late-night project.

Precise:
Roger consumed the food.
The manager reduced the prices.
Kristin coordinated the late-night project.

Vivid:
Roger devoured the food.
The manager slashed the prices.
Kristin plunged into her late-night project.

Passive voice is appropriate only when the actor is unknown, unimportant, or obvious, and there is no need for a strong, precise, or vivid verb.

Admission is refunded only when the performance is interrupted before the intermission.

The parcels have been shipped to your address.

acute, chronic

When referring to pain, disease, or illness, *acute* means sharp or immediate, while *chronic* means ongoing and does not indicate severity.

adapt, adept, adopt

Adapt means to adjust or alter.

Dream Theater adapted to cult stardom by offering special performances and recordings to hardcore fans outside of normal marketing channels.

Adept, the adjective, means skillful or proficient. *Adept*, the noun, means one who is skillful or proficient. It is correct to say John

Myung is adept at playing the bass guitar and also correct to say John Myung is a bass guitar adept.

Adopt means to take the position or status of another as one's own, without change or exception.

The band adopted their new label's plan to release studio videos to promote the album.

The committee adopted the contractor's plan to repair the roof of the meeting hall before installing the new floor.

addresses

Abbreviate state names in addresses using the two-letter postal code. *CA*, not *California*, *Calif.* or *Cal.*

Abbreviate compass directions: *4 N. Privet Lane*

Use numerals in numeric street names: *505 N. 16th Street*; the *59th Street Bridge*

Use one space after the state abbreviation and the ZIP code: *Beverly Hills, CA 90210*

Use the following format when listing a professional contact and address, including punctuation thus:

Name: Jean Valjean
Address: Alaska Department of Corrections
24601 N. Prison Circle
Remote City, AK 99999
Telephone: (888)555-1212
Fax: (888)555-1213
E-mail: jvaljean@alaskadoc.gov

admissible

Spelled thus. *Admissable* looks correct, but is not.

adverbs

Place an adverb before the word modified to ensure the correct meaning is communicated. For creative writing, stronger verbs are better than adverbs.

Right: Jordan Rudess played quickly through the piano solo.

Better: Jordan Rudess blasted through the piano solo.

For professional writing, such as instructional documents, statutory or regulatory drafting, or contract formation, adverbs may be more precise, and a creative verb may not be appropriate.

Right: Submit the required data as soon as possible.

Wrong: Dispatch the required data right away.

Better: Immediately submit the required data.

adverse, averse

Not synonymous. *Adverse* means contrary or hostile, while *averse* means opposed to or disinclined to something.

The real-estate agent found it difficult to sell the Colvin ranch house in today's adverse market conditions, but he was averse to reducing the price because that would minimize his commission.

advice, advise, inform

Advice means suggestions or recommendations concerning a course of action. *Advise* means to offer counsel and suggestions. *Inform* means to communicate information.

The band's management advises them on publicity decisions. On the manager's advice, the band decided to inform the fans that the tour was postponed for three months.

affect, effect

Affect means to influence (usually a verb):

The slowing economy affected album sales.

Effect means result (usually a noun):

The effect of the slowing economy was a reduction in album sales.

afterward

Not *afterwards*.

ages

Always use numerals. Ages expressed as adjectives before a noun or as substitutes for a noun use hyphens. A 12-year-old girl. The girl is 12 years old. The show is for 7-year-olds.

airtight

Compound words eventually lose hyphenation through usage. Compare *watertight*.

alternate, alternative

Alternate means a substitute. *Alternative* means a choice between two or more possibilities.

alternately, alternatively

Alternately is an adverb that means *in turn; one after the other*:

Each member of the band alternately took center stage to perform a solo piece.

Alternatively is an adverb that means *on the other hand, one or the other*:

You can buy the new Dream Theater album at a record store, or, alternatively, you can purchase a digital copy online.

altogether, all together

All together is applied to people or things that are being treated as a group.

The band members appeared all together in the publicity photograph.

All together is the form that must be used if the sentence can be reworded so that all and together are separated by other words:

The band members all appeared together in the publicity photograph.

All the band members appeared together in the publicity photograph.

Altogether is used to mean entirely:

Mike Portnoy was altogether pleased to be inducted into the Modern Drummer Hall of Fame.

aluminum

Spelled thus. *Aluminium* is the British spelling.

a.m. and p.m.

See **time**.

amid

Not *amidst*. Thou art not composing in High Style.

among, between

Among is used when things are shared by more than two people. *Between* is used when things are shared by two.

The revenue from album sales is divided among the five band members.

The left end of the stage is split between John Myung and Jordan Rudess.

amount, number

Amount tells *how much*. *Number* tells *how many*.

Compare the number of tickets Dream Theater sold with the amount the band earned in ticket sales.

ampersand (&)

Use the ampersand when it is part of a formal name:

Emerson Lake & Palmer
Proctor & Gamble
The acoustic covers of Pipo & Elo

Do not use the ampersand in place of *and*.

and/or

Do not use *and/or*. The meaning of *or*, by itself, is inclusive of the possibility of *and*. Use *or* when one or more conditions apply, and use *and* when all conditions apply.

annul

Means *to make null* and is a derivative of *null*. The British spelling retains the second l while the American spelling discards it.

another

Another is not a synonym for *additional*. It refers to an element that duplicates a previously stated quantity.

Right: Ten people came backstage; another 10 were turned away.

Wrong: Ten people came backstage; another 20 were turned away.

Right: Ten people came backstage; 20 others were turned away.

anticipate, expect

Anticipate means to expect and prepare for something; *expect* does not include the notion of preparation.

Dream Theater expected record crowds on their first visit to Chile. They anticipated the high turnout by booking large, spacious venues.

anti-abortion
anticrime
antipollution

Though compound words lose hyphenation gradually through usage, the prevailing usage of some prefixes can be inconsistent. Guessing incorrectly on whether to hyphenate an *anti-* term will have less impact on a document as long as the usage is internally consistent throughout the document.

apostrophes

Incorrect apostrophe usage is one of the clarion signals indicating that a document is written unprofessionally. Apostrophes used correctly are invisible, while apostrophes used incorrectly stand out like a banana in a box of oranges. Learning correct apostrophe usage is even more critical than the correct usage of *that* and *which* and proper handling of abbreviations.

The simple rule is that an apostrophe is used for possession or contraction, but *never* to make a word plural. The outlying case is *its/it's*, which has its own rule.

POSSESSION: John Petrucci's guitar. Mike Portnoy's drumming skills. The band members' tour luggage.

QUASI-POSSESSION: One week's time. Seven days' pay.

CONTRACTION: See **contractions**.

Plurals never use an apostrophe, even when the item being pluralized is a letter, abbreviation, symbol, or figure:

Mark the attendance sheet with Xs.

Dream Theater has released nine albums and six concert DVDs.

The band was formed in 1985, but first became prominent in the 1990s.

But: The Oakland A's baseball club. This is correct because *A 's* is a contraction for *Athletics*. The letter *A* is not plural; the word *Athletics* is plural, and *A* is its contraction.

ITS/IT'S: The one instance where possession does not use an apostrophe is with *its*. *It's* is only used when *it is* could be substituted:

Right: The painting was mounted in its own frame.

Wrong: The painting was mounted in it's own frame.

The first example looks wrong, but is correct. The second example looks right, but is more clearly understood to be wrong by substituting:

Wrong: The painting was mounted in *it is* own frame.

appendix

An appendix should only be used for reference material sufficiently corollary to the primary document that including the material in the main body of the text would be disruptive. A good test to determine whether the material is corollary is to examine whether the document would be substantively complete if the appendix did not exist.

Appendices may also restate substance from the main body of the document in an easier-to-reference format, such as in a table or chart. Such a table or chart can even contain entries not referenced in the main body of the text, and would still be properly corollary. The main text of a document about waterfowl populations, for example, could contain an appendix with a table of all ornithological species. The main text conveys its intended analysis of waterfowl, and the appendix offers extra context to anyone curious to know how the facts and figures from the main text compare to those of other related species.

apposition

A decision on whether to put commas around a word, phrase, or clause used in apposition depends on whether it is essential to the meaning of the sentence (no commas) or not essential (use commas).

Right: Vocalist James LaBrie, the frontman for Dream Theater, first appeared on the album *Images and Words* in 1992.

Right: Vocalist James LaBrie of Dream Theater first appeared on the album *Images and Words* in 1992.

Wrong: Vocalist James LaBrie, of Dream Theater, first appeared on the album *Images and Words* in 1992.

approximately

See **about, approximately**.

average of

The phrase takes a plural verb in a construction such as:

An average of 500 fans are browsing the Dream Theater online message boards on any given day.

This is correct, but is often flagged (wrongly) by software.

averse, adverse

See **adverse, averse**

awhile, a while

Mike Portnoy will drum awhile. Mike Portnoy plans to drum for a while.

B

back up (v.), backup (n., adj.)

Back up your data. Use the external *backup* drive. The external drive will be your data *backup*.

backward

Not *backwards*.

balance, remainder

Balance is used in business to mean the amount still owned after a partial payment or the excess of debits over credits. *Remainder* is what is left when a part is taken away.

because, since

Use *because* to denote a specific cause-effect relationship:

Dream Theater was stuck at a midtown Manhattan studio for a week because the events of September 11, 2001 resulted in the closure of all roadways out of the city.

Since is acceptable in a causal sense when the first event in a sequence led logically to the second but was not its direct cause:

They went to the concert, since they had been given the tickets.

(Replacing *since* with *because* in this example gives a different meaning.)

Since also refers to something that happened at a particular time in the past. Do not use *since* when you mean *because*.

The band has not performed "You Not Me" since the Falling Into Infinity tour in 1998.

beside, besides

Beside means *at the side of*; *right next to*.

Jordan's keyboard stood beside his effects rack.

Besides means *in addition to*.

Jordan has plenty of audio gear besides his keyboard and effects rack, such as his Continuum Fingerboard.

biannually, biennially

Biannually means twice a year.

Dream Theater divides marketing royalties among the band members biannually: once in June and once in December.

Biennially means every two years.

Dream Theater has toured roughly biennially since the late 1990s.

bimonthly, semimonthly

Bimonthly means every other month. *Semimonthly* means twice a month.

bipartisan

Spelled thus, and not hyphenated. Appropriate for use whenever presumably separate blocs behave similarly or cooperate.

The bipartisan crowd of classic progressive rock fans cheered as loudly for the opening set by Dream Theater as they did for the headline set by Yes.

biweekly

Not strictly a synonym for *semimonthly*, though in practice it may mean almost the same thing. Non-leap Februaries last exactly four weeks, and every other month is slightly longer. Typically, employees paid biweekly have 26 paychecks in a year, while employees paid semimonthly have 24.

bookmaking

Compound words eventually lose hyphenation through usage. Most commonly used as an adjective in its compound form and as separate words otherwise:

A bookmaking organization is not interested in book making, but instead accepts wagers on the outcomes of sporting events.

book titles

See **italics**.

buildup (n.), build up (v.)

The military buildup prior to the invasion took three months.

It took Kevin Moore eight years to build up the desire to leave the band.

bulkhead

The nautical term for *interior wall*. Useful metaphorically for any device or method that cleanly and securely partitions an enclosed area.

bus, buses

The verb forms: *bus, bused, busing. Busses* is a synonym for *kisses*, and *bussing* is a synonym for *kissing*.

businessperson

Preferred to businessman in formal communication.
See **gender-specific terminology**.

bylaw (n.), by law (adverbial usage)

A list of organizational bylaws is an incorporation requirement by law.

bypass (n., v.)

The tour bus had to approach the arena via the freeway bypass.

John Petrucci bypasses his effects rack to play a clean, unaltered tone.

byproduct (n.)

Compound words eventually lose hyphenation through usage.

byway

Obsolete style superseded by *route*. Most commonly seen in transportation documents from the mid-20th century, in which branch routes off the interstate system were often named *scenic byways*. Today, use *scenic route* in almost all cases, and use *bypass* to indicate the supersession of the prevailing road.

Historic Route 66 has been bypassed or replaced by interstates for much of its length, but still exists as a scenic route through parts of northern New Mexico and Arizona, including a stop at the Grand Canyon trailhead in Peach Springs.

C

cancel, canceled, canceling, cancellation

Many word processing spelling filters fail to catch the incorrect *cancelled*, which is a leftover artifact of the previous British usage.

The band had no choice: James suffered from bronchitis, so three concerts had to be canceled.

cannot

Not contracted.

capital, capitol

Capital as a noun means an uppercase letter, site of government, or money. *Capitol* means the main government building. *Capital* as an adjective is British slang for wonderful or excellent, or, in American and British military usage, a designation for a primary or most important vessel:

The convoy lost its destroyers and supply tenders, but at least the capital ships were intact: both battleships and the aircraft carrier survived the enemy attack.

capitalization

Spelled thus both for upper-case letters and for the process of acquiring investment funds for a business venture.

Do not capitalize *rule*, *law*, *state*, or *federal* unless the word is part of an official name of an agency, an act, an organization, or some other proper noun.

Do not capitalize *federal government* or *government* when referring specifically to the United States government. In formal documents where those words are intended to have the force of an official name, they may be capitalized.

Capitalize titles of individuals when they precede a person's name (Senator Baynes) but not when they follow the person's name (Edward Baynes, senator).

Match the capitalization and formatting of proper nouns and trademarks: eBay, SportsCenter, WalMart, EastWest Records, iMac, iPod, tool (the band from California).

cardholder

Compound words eventually lose hyphenation through usage. Much more prevalent today, this usage was rarely seen before the digital age. In the mid-20th century, people did not *hold* cards, but instead *carried* cards. Hence, the slang phrase a card-carrying Communist.

caregiver
caretaker
carpool
carryforward (n.)

Compound words eventually lose hyphenation through usage.

carryout (n., adj.)

Different from *carry out*, which is used as a verb.

Do you want carryout tonight?

She went to pick up the carryout dinner.

I need to carry out the trash.

carryover (n.)

Different from *carry over*, which is used as a verb.

The carryover from last year's budget is $51,000.

We will carry over $51,000 from last year's budget.

caseworker, case worker

Either form is acceptable, as long as it is used consistently.

CD-ROM

Not *CDROM*. The term is ubiquitous, so only extremely formal technically-oriented documents would require it be spelled out as *compact disc: read-only memory*.

cement

Cement is the powder mixed with water and sand or gravel to make *concrete*. The proper term is *concrete* (not cement) *pavement*, *block*, or *foundation*.

check

In Banking, spelled thus. Not *cheque*, which is an artifact of British spelling still occasionally (and incorrectly) seen in American usage.

checklist

Common enough that *check list* would be improper usage.

checkout (n., adj.)

Not used as a verb.

I brought the CDs to the checkout counter.

I purchased the CDs through the online checkout.

But:

I wanted to check out the new Dream Theater CD.

checkup (n., adj.)

Not used as a verb.

I went to the doctor for my checkup examination.
The doctor gave me a thorough checkup.

But:

I visited the library to check up on my source material.

chronic, acute

See **acute, chronic**.

cipher

Spelled thus, and meaning an *empty set* or *nullity*. *Cypher* is a British variant. Richard Cypher is the main character in Terry Goodkind's novel series *The Sword of Truth*.

cleanup (n., adj.)

Not used as a verb. Hyphenation is still acceptable in adjective use.

I participated in the cleanup project.

I participated in the clean-up project.

The cleanup of the campground took six hours.

But:

It took six hours to clean up the campground.

clearinghouse

This term is seeing increasingly common usage in the contexts of electronic monetary transactions and medical insurance. Virtually never seen as separate words except in the outmoded *Publishers' Clearing House*.

codefendant

Hyphenation is still occasionally seen, but is outdated usage. See also **legal pleading style**.

colons

Use a colon between two independent clauses when the second clause explains or illustrates the first clause and there is no coordinating conjunction or transitional expression linking the two clauses.

The new rules will simplify filing: only electronic submissions will be required.

Use colons to introduce a list or an example. Do not use a colon when a form of the verb *to be* is used.

The three courses required in this program are accounting, business English, and Computer Science.

Do not use a colon between two independent clauses when the two clauses are equal in value. Use a semi-colon or period instead. See **semi-colons**.

commas

When in doubt, do not use a comma. A comma omitted can be assumed inadvertent, while a comma wrongly included can only be assumed intentional.

Use a comma to separate independent clauses in a compound sentence.

Use a comma to separate three or more items in a series. The prevailing usage other than in newspaper media is to serialize the comma after every item in the list:

Dream Theater's 1992 lineup included James LaBrie, John Petrucci, John Myung, Mike Portnoy, and Kevin Moore.

Do not separate a month and year with a comma: *January 2009*. See **lists** and **semi-colons** and **apposition**.

commingle

Do not be tempted to write *co-mingle*, even though the word is pronounced that way.

committeeperson

Correct usage. See **gender-specific terminology**.

communitywide

Sometimes hyphenated, but the prevailing usage is a compound word.

complement, compliment

Complement is a noun and a verb denoting completeness or the process of supplementing something:

The road crew had a complement of 54 employees.
Mike Portnoy's beard complements his shaggy mane of hair.

Compliment is a noun or verb that denotes praise:

The band complimented the roadies for efficient work on the third leg of the tour.

complementary, complimentary

The tax attorney and her husband, an accountant, have complementary careers.

Members of the band's Japanese fan club were given complimentary backstage passes.

compose, comprise, constitute

Compose means to create or put together.

Dream Theater is composed of five musicians.

Comprise means to contain or to include all.

Dream Theater's 2008 concert tour schedule comprised 125 cities.

Constitute may be preferable to *compose* or *comprise* when the intended meaning is that the subject elements make up the entirety of the object.

Ten buses and six trucks constitute the band's touring transportation equipment.

compound words

Compound words usually begin as two separate words with one space between the two words. With frequent use, a hyphen may be added to link them together. When the use of the hyphenated compound word becomes common, the hyphen is usually dropped. See **hyphen**.

comprise, constitute, compose

See **compose, comprise, constitute**.

concurrent, consecutive

Consecutive means successive:

Dream Theater released DVDs after three consecutive albums: *Live at Budokan* after *Train of Thought*, *Score* after *Octavarium*, and *Chaos in Motion* after *Systematic Chaos*.

Concurrent is an adjective that means simultaneous:

The *Score* DVD and live CD were released concurrently.

connote

Connote is a verb that means to imply or suggest:

The term *progressive metal* connotes epic concept albums and lengthy instrumental flourishes.

Denote is a verb that means to indicate or refer to specifically:

The slang term *prog* denotes the combined progressive metal and progressive rock genres.

consistency

Make the reader's job easier by choosing terms the same way each time they are used. Don't use different words to denote the same thing.

Wrong: Each employee shall notify the band manager if the crewmember is unavailable for the next leg of the tour.

Right: Each employee shall notify the band manager if the employee is unavailable for the next leg of the tour.

Also, don't use the same word to denote different things.

Wrong: The band will stage the show from a 250-square-foot stage.

Right: The band will perform the show from a 250-square-foot stage.

constitute, compose, comprise

See **compose, comprise, constitute**.

contiguous, continual, continuous

Contiguous means adjoining in space, touching.

The suite *Six Degrees of Inner Turbulence* consists of eight contiguous songs.

Continual means something that happens again and again, over a long period of time.

Insatiable fan demand has prompted Dream Theater's continual touring.

Continuous means without interruption, steady, unbroken.

The second European leg of the tour included a continuous stretch of 18 days without a break.

contractions

Do not use contractions in writing, except for dialogue when writing fiction, and in general usage when the audience is likely to be very informal. In addition to reducing the clarity and understandability of your text, contractions can make your document more difficult to translate into other languages.

convince, persuade

One *convinces* a person that something is true but *persuades* a person to do something.

Insisting that the theaters would sell out, the Australian fans persuaded their local concert promoters to book Dream Theater in Melbourne, Sydney, and Adelaide. After tickets sold out within minutes, the promoters were convinced that booking the shows was a good idea.

Following this rule, *convince* should not be used with an infinitive.

Wrong: Concert promoters in Australia, encouraged by the band's success, were convinced to schedule more shows on the band's subsequent tour.

Right: Concert promoters in Australia, encouraged by the band's success, were persuaded to schedule more shows on the band's subsequent tour.

copayment

This usage is increasingly prevalent with the emergence of health care policy as a mainstream political issue.

council, counsel

Council means a group of people. *Counsel* means an attorney, advice, or to advise. A *councilor* is a member of a *council*, and a *counselor* is one who *counsels*.

The village council counseled the alleged assailant to retain counsel on his own behalf. After the man was convicted, he was ordered to visit a counselor for rehabilitation.

creditworthiness

This usage is increasingly prevalent with the collapse of the mortgage industry and the reduction of liquidity in the marketplace in 2008.

criterion, criteria

Criterion is the singular, *criteria* the plural. There is no such thing as *fulfilling a criteria*. That would read the same as *eating a sandwiches*. Instead use *fulfilling the criteria* or *fulfilling all criteria*.

cross section (n.) cross-section (v.)

Spelled thus, and hyphenated only in verb usage.

D

dash

Use a dash for two separate independent clauses when you intend them to be interrupted by a pause in reading, such as with a character's internal monologue in fiction:

The train station was still four blocks away -- I hoped I was running fast enough.

Most modern word processing software automatically formats a dash into a longer version of a hyphen. Be careful of dash usage, because editing of text does not always preserve the automatic formatting and a semi-colon or parentheses might be more appropriate punctuation.

Common usage in typing when automatic formatting is not available or is disabled is to type two hyphens "--" instead of a dash. This is acceptable as long as it is consistent throughout the document. A single hyphen will usually be mistaken for a hyphen. See also **parentheses, semi-colons.**

dates

When writing dates, spell out the date rather than writing it in numerical form. See commas.

Wrong: 9/11/01
Right: September 11, 2001

Wrong: 8/08
Right: August 2008 (no comma)

decades

Use Arabic numerals to indicate decades of history. Use an apostrophe to indicate missing numerals, not to pluralize. Pluralize by adding the letter *s*: the 1970s, the '40s, the mid-1990s.

defuse, diffuse

See **diffuse, defuse**.

degrees

Use the degree symbol.

Wrong: 102 degrees Fahrenheit
Right: 102° F (space before the F and no period after the F); 35° C

dependent

(Noun and adjective.) Not *dependant*. A *dependent* (noun form) is a person who is supported financially by another person. A *pendant* is a piece of jewelry.

different

Use with the preposition *from*, not *than*.

Dream Theater's previous vocalist, Charlie Dominici, sported an operatic style different from James LaBrie's aggressive, vivid tones.

diffuse, defuse

Not synonymous. To *diffuse* means to disperse and scatter. To *defuse* means to remove the firing mechanism from a bomb or otherwise render a dangerous situation safe.

directness; imperative mood

When writing instructions, rules, regulations, statutes, orders, guidelines, or checklists, direct the language to the reader to make your meaning clear, concise, and understandable. This helps avoid inadvertent use of the passive voice. Examples:

Sign each page.

Attach a photograph to the file.

Arrive at the west entrance by 9:00 a.m.

Prepare the instruments for sound check at least two hours before the doors are scheduled to open.

disassemble, dissemble

Not synonymous. To *disassemble* means to take apart. To *dissemble* means to tell lies.

discreet, discrete

Discreet is an adjective that means prudent, circumspect, or modest:

The band quietly enjoyed dinner in the back room of the restaurant, depending on their server to be discreet by not drawing attention to their presence.

Discrete is an adjective that means separate or individually distinct:

Each member of the band has a discrete sound channel fed to his in-ear monitor, ensuring that he can hear his own performance clearly even under poor acoustical conditions.

disinterested, uninterested

Disinterested is an adjective that means *unbiased* or *impartial*:

The referee's call upset the fans, but both coaches knew he was a disinterested party and meant no unfair advantage to accrue to either of them.

Uninterested is an adjective that means *not interested* or *indifferent*:

Mechanic Records seemed uninterested in allowing Dream Theater to buy out their original contract and recording rights.

donut

Spelled thus. *Doughnut* has all but left American usage.

Dream Theater

Dream Theater is a progressive-metal musical band from New York. The band's history was so flavorful and interesting that it made an ideal subject for the example phrases in this book.

E

each

Takes a singular verb.

each other, one another

Two guitarists admire each other. More than two admire one another. More than five or so and you can forget about getting anything done in the practice room for the rest of the day.

earthmoving

Not hyphenated, and used thus mainly when referring to utility vehicles and equipment.

eBay

Capitalized thus. See **capitalization**.

economic, economical

Not synonymous. *Economic* means having to do with the economy. *Economical* means *financially prudent* or *frugal*, such as with money, or *sparing in use*, such as with time or language.

effect, affect

See **affect, effect.**

e-mail

Lowercase in the middle of a sentence, but capitalize the *e* when it stands alone as a designating tag:

E-mail: rossedwardsbooks@gmail.com.

Do not underline or italicize an e-mail address.

embarrassed

Using two *r* and two *s* when you spell this word will prevent you from experiencing this word when you submit your document.

eminent, imminent

Not synonymous. *Eminent* means *highly regarded.* *Imminent* means *about to occur.*

ensure, insure, assure

Use *ensure* to mean *guarantee*:

The promoter hired security staff to ensure a safe, trouble-free concert.

Use *insure* for references to insurance:

The promoter bought a policy to insure against losses if the crowd got out of control and forced a cancellation of the concert.

Assure is an acceptable synonym for *ensure*, but is most appropriately used as a verb:

The promoter assured the band that crowd control would not present any problems.

entitled

Use it to mean a *right* to do something or to have something. Do not use it to mean *titled*.

Dream Theater's first studio album was titled *When Dream and Day Unite*.

ESPN

Not an abbreviation and therefore never written out in a document. Originally the *Entertainment and Sports Network*. See also **capitalization** (SportsCenter).

exacerbate, exasperate

Not synonymous. To *exacerbate* means to make worse. To *exasperate* means to exhaust one's tolerance.

The raining drizzle exacerbated the electrical problems that dogged the sound technicians.

By the end of the night, the soundboard controller was exasperated by the repeated equipment failures.

except, accept

See **accept, except.**

exceptions

Avoid starting a sentence with an exception. Exceptions in general are best to express through the natural language of a statement, rather than setting the exceptions aside, unless doing so would result in a long or cumbersome list or elaborate description.

Wrong: Sunday, Monday, Tuesday, Thursday, and Saturday will be the band's practice days.
Right: The band will practice every day except Wednesday and Friday.

Note that the sentence first establishes the category *every day* and then states the exceptions.

F

Fahrenheit (F)

See **degree**.

farmworker

For extremely formal usage, the ubiquitous *farmer* is not technically correct. Anywhere else, just use *farmer*.

farther, further

Farther refers to physical distance that can be measured.

Further means *to a greater degree or extent* and refers to matters in which physical measurement is impossible or in which distance is figurative.

The band hoped that touring farther from home would result in further album and merchandise sales.

fax (n., v.)

Preferred over *facsimile*.

federal government

Lowercase in all uses.

fewer, less

In general, use *fewer* for individual items, *less* for bulk or quantity.

Wrong: The trend is toward less people in attendance. She was fewer than 18 years old.
Right: Fewer than 50 tickets remain available. He had less than $20 in his wallet.

firefighter

Not *fireman*. Firefighters may be of any gender.

firefighting

Generally used as an adjective to describe the equipment used by firefighters. The verb usage is more properly phrased *fighting fires*.

firehouse

Firehouse achieved platinum album sales and critical acclaim in 1991 on the heels of their hit ballad *Love of a Lifetime*.

fireproof

Not hyphenated. Compare *waterproof*.

flammable, inflammable

These two words are actually synonyms, both meaning *easily set on fire*. Though both are used on either side of the Atlantic, *inflammable* is prevalent in British usage, while *flammable* dominates American usage.

John Myung had to be sure his shirt contained no flammable material, because he would be standing close to the pyrotechnic devices during the encore.

flaunt, flout

To *flaunt* means to show off shamelessly:

Derek Sherinian flaunted his solo keyboarding skills during the *Awake* tour because he knew Dream Theater's audience expected him to prove himself.

To *flout* means to show scorn or contempt for:

The band flouted the mainstream media by refusing to compromise their musical style.

floodplain

Never hyphenated, but acceptable either compound or as separate words.

footnotes

The type of document you are writing will determine whether you use footnotes, endnotes, or inline citations. Generally, do not mix more than one type. For a term paper using footnotes, use only footnotes. For a dissertation using endnotes, use only endnotes.

Legal memoranda, law school writing, and related documents typically use inline citations. Legal analyses and rulings sometimes mix inline citations and endnotes, but the prevailing usage is only inline citations. Legal pleadings in many jurisdictions are now required by format and style rules to use inline citations exclusively.

forward

Not *forwards*.

founder, flounder

In its primary sense *founder* means to sink below the surface of the water:

The boat foundered under the weight of too much cargo.

By extension, *founder* means to fail entirely:

Mechanic Records' underdeveloped marketing plan for *When Dream and Day Unite* foundered, leaving the band without a promotional tour.

Flounder means to move about clumsily or to act with confusion, synonymously with *blunder*:

After Steve Stone floundered his way through the first set in a 1990 club show, Dream Theater was so embarrassed that they fired him during the intermission.

fractions

Spell out a fraction at the beginning of a sentence. For most uses, use Arabic numbers: 6 2/3, 1/2 inch, 1/8 mile.

Spell out when a fraction detracts from readability: the first half of the year.

Do not use a hyphen to separate a whole number from a fraction: 8 1/2" by 11".

Do not use fraction symbols. These symbols sometimes disappear if your document is converted to one file type or another, when certain font changes are applied, and when your text is copied-and-pasted to certain word processing software suites.
See **ordinals and numbers**.

freestanding

Always an adjective form:

The monument is a freestanding structure.

freshwater

Compound words eventually lose hyphenation through usage.

full time, full-time

Hyphenate when used as a compound modifier (adjective phrasing):

She works full time. He has a full-time job.

further, farther

See **farther, further**.

G

gay

Synonymous with *happy*, but that meaning is rarely seen in present-day usage. Use *gay* only when you mean *homosexual*, whether in noun or adjective phrasing. Do not combine or substitute *gay* with slang or jargon.

gender-specific terminology

Do not use words that unnecessarily distinguish between male and female. Use *police officer*, not *policeman* or *policewoman*.

Avoid the gender-specific pronoun when the antecedent could be male or female.

Wrong: The supervisor or his designee shall approve all new hires.
Right: The supervisor or the supervisor's designee shall approve all new hires.

Be careful when you rewrite to avoid the problem. The following examples do not necessarily have the same meaning:

Each Vice President shall submit his or her recommendations to the Board of Directors.

The Vice Presidents shall submit their recommendations to the Board of Directors.

Do not attempt to avoid using a gender-specific pronoun by using a plural pronoun with a singular noun.

Wrong: The student shall submit their research paper.
Right: The student shall submit the student's research paper.

Do not use *s/he*, *he/she*, or *his or her*.

Avoid:	Use:
chairman	chair, chairperson
crewman	crew member
draftsman	drafter
fireman	firefighter
foreman	supervisor
man-hours	hours worked, staff-hours
mankind	humanity, humankind
manpower	personnel, workforce
policeman	police officer

government

Lowercase *government* unless it is part of a formal title: the U.S. government, the state government, the United States Government Accounting Office.

grammar

Use *a* or *an* when you mean any item or individual. Use *the* when referring to a specific subject already described.

Avoid split infinitives. Do not write *to always go* or *to slowly climb*. Write instead *always to go* or *slowly to climb* or *to climb slowly*.

Make the verb agree with its subject in number and person. The following words are singular and take a singular verb:

Anyone, anybody, each, everyone, everybody, either, no one, nobody, neither, one, somebody, someone.

The following words referring to groups take a singular verb:

Audience, family, kind, band, flock, lot, class, group, number, committee, heap, none, crowd, herd, public, dozen, jury, team.

The following words are plural and take a plural verb:

Media, data, criteria, phenomena.

Do not use contractions. Write out each verb.

gray

Not *grey*. But: *greyhound*. *Grey's Anatomy* is an ABC television drama marketed primarily toward female viewers.

groundwater

Not hyphenated even when used as an adjective:
The surveyors detected groundwater contamination.

group

Takes singular verbs and pronouns: The group is waiting in the after-show lounge.

H

handgun

Never used with a hyphen anymore.

harass, harassment

There is only one *r* in the spelling of any form of the word.

health care

Two words.

historic, historical

In general usage, *historic* refers to what is important in history, while *historical* applies more broadly to whatever existed in the past whether it was important or not:

The historic treaty ended the war.
Historical buildings will be razed to make room for freeway construction.

Do not use the article *an* before the word *history*, *historic*, or *historical*. Use *a*. The infrequent remaining usage of *an* before *historic* and its derivatives is British.

horsepower

Spelled thus and never hyphenated.

hyphens

Use hyphens to connect words:

Nouns: sister-in-law, follow-up, one-third

Verbs: double-space, tape-record

Compound adjectives appearing before a noun: all-inclusive list, black-and-white picture, decision-making authority, long-range goals, full-time employees, up-to-date record.

Use a hyphen when two or more words act together to create a new meaning.

Use a hyphen when the first part of a compound adjective contains a number: third-party liability, two-party system.

Use a hyphen after a prefix when the prefix precedes a capitalized word: pre-World War I.

Do not use a hyphen between adverbs ending in -ly and adjectives they modify: a fully informed applicant, a badly damaged foundation.

See **suspensive hyphenation** and **compound words.**

I

if, whether

If introduces a conditional clause. *Whether* introduces a noun clause involving choices.

imminent, eminent

See **eminent, imminent**.

imperative mood

See **directness, imperative mood**.

imply, infer

Not synonymous. A speaker *implies* when he suggests additional meaning. A listener *infers* when he draws additional meaning from what is said. A speaker never *infers*, and a listener never *implies*.

When Lucia said she was hungry, she was implying that Grady should make dinner.

When Lucia said she was hungry, Grady inferred that she wanted him to make dinner.

inappropriate words

Because of the need for precision, certain words should be avoided other than in written dialogue:

Can should be used only to indicate ability, not permission.

Should and *could* are poor usage and should be avoided, especially in legal writing.

Will is used only in limited circumstances, such as when *shall* forms a cumbersome phrase.

Do not use *must*; use *shall* instead.

May is used to indicate discretion. When using *may*, specify the standards under which that discretion is given, unless it is trivial.

The venue manager may give backstage passes to fans who appear clean and orderly and who are wearing the band's apparel.

The venue's security staff may deny entry and refund the cost of admission to anyone.

include

Use *include* to introduce a series when the items that follow are only part of the total:

Dream Theater's breakthrough album *Images and Words* included the rock-radio mainstays *Pull Me Under* and *Take the Time*.

Use *comprise* when the full list on individual elements is given:

The album *Images and Words* comprises eight songs spanning a total of approximately one hour.

indispensable

Spelled thus. *Indispensible* looks and sounds correct, but is not.

indoor (adj.), indoors (adv.)

He plays indoor basketball. He went indoors.

infant

Applicable to children from birth to 12 months old. A 13-month-old child is a *toddler*.

infer, imply

See **imply, infer**.

infrared
infrastructure

The prefix *infra-* is pronounced *in-fra*, not *in-fer* or *in-fera*.

inoculate

Very commonly misspelled as *innoculate*.

interagency
interoffice
international
interstate

Spelled thus and generally not hyphenated. The prefix *inter-* means *between or among more than one of* the type of entity identified in the suffix. See also **intrastate**.

internet

Lowercase *i*. Style guides as recently as the 1990s still capitalize the word, but that usage is no longer correct. Within the context of a phrase mentioning the internet, common computer-based abbreviations are acceptable, within reason:

The annual report is posted on the internet in HTML, PDF, and RTF formats.

intramural
intrastate
intravenous

Spelled thus and generally not hyphenated. The prefix *intra-* means *within a single one of* the type of entity identified in the suffix. See also **interstate**.

irony

Irony is a discrepancy between what is said or understood and what actually happens:

The President said that we must protect the peace, but, ironically, he ordered the military buildup to continue.

In literary expression, irony can also be an incongruity between what is said and what is meant:

The Devil demanded Leela's hand in payment for his favor. Leela thought she had to sacrifice part of her body, but the Devil, ironically, actually meant that he wanted "her hand in marriage."

Irony is not synonymous for coincidence, misfortune, or happenstance.

Wrong: Rain on one's wedding day is ironic.
Wrong: A free ride when one has already paid is ironic.
Wrong: Good advice that one just did not take is ironic.
Right: A song about irony containing examples that are not ironic is ironic.

irregardless

A double negative. *Regardless* is correct.

italics

Italicization varies more widely by document type than most other rules, so for formal documents, it is best to consult the applicable style guide. For general usage, place the following in italics:

Titles of books, films, plays, or other creative or instructional works: *Star Wars, The Grapes of Wrath, Les Miserables*

Scientific names: *homo sapiens, canis lupus*

The name of a legal case: *Miranda* v. *Arizona* (the v. is not in italics)
See also **style guides**.

J

jargon, technical language, foreign phrases, legalese, and other inappropriate language

Use plain English unless your audience is absolutely, positively limited to people who will understand your jargon or technical phrases as second nature. It is even advisable to minimize its use in those situations because the use of jargon varies between groups: some publishers say that a newly-released book *drops* on Tuesday, while others say it *lands* on Tuesday. The plainer the English, the less confusing the material is to the reader.

Unlike legitimate technical terms, which outsiders could look up in a dictionary, jargon is a private language that has meaning only to a particular group. If these special words or phrases are necessary to the understanding of your text, define the jargon clearly up front.

Avoid redundant phrases, long sentences, passive voice, and topic-specific acronyms unless you first define each one. Use concrete or common use words and phrases, and make sentences short, direct, and clear.

Do not add -ize to a noun to make it into a verb. A pointy-haired boss does that, and everybody at the conference table discovers that he or she is an idiot.

Do not use a foreign phrase if an everyday English equivalent can be used. This applies in any context from simple to advanced:

Use *meet* instead of *rendezvous*.
Use *plot device* instead of *scenes-a-faire*.

Use *impolite behavior* instead of *schadenfreude*.
Use *business association* instead of *keiretsu*.

Avoid unclear words and phrases that sound like legalese:
aforesaid, hereby, hereinabove, pursuant to, said, such, thereof, thereunto, to wit, whatsoever, and *wherein.*

judgment

Not the British spelling *judgement*.

K

kindergarten

Spelled thus. Not *kindergarden*. A common misspelling because the word means literally *childrens' garden* in German.

L

laid, lain, lay

Laid is the past tense and the past participle of the verb *lay* and not the past tense of *lie*. *Lay* is the past tense of the verb *lie* and *lain* is the past participle:

She laid her equipment down and lay down on the bed, where she has lain for an hour.

Latin words

Italicize scientific names in Latin. Do not italicize Latin phrases (such as ad hoc, et seq., ex parte, de jure). Unless your document is legal, medical, or scientific, avoid using Latin phrases at all.

legal pleading style

Many jurisdictions impose local style guidelines. Beyond those requirements, generally speaking, the modern usage taught today in law schools applies, utilizing direct, minimalist phrasing. Style guides such as the Bluebook and the ALWD Manual have been updated to reflect the modern usage. The legal pleading style taught in law schools until the 1980s is now considered archaic and wasteful. If your jurisdiction does not impose a style requirement for a given component of your document, it is best to default to current usage and avoid legalese.

Wrong (old form): COMES NOW the plaintiff, Buckwheat Thomas, by and through counsel undersigned, and does plead this court for the fullest redress of grievances for harms caused by and through the defendants and co-defendants, and each of them, among which stand at least John David Stutts. The plaintiff herein and hereby alleges said harms as follows, to wit:...

Right (new form): Plaintiff Buckwheat Thomas suffered bullet impact injuries caused by the negligence of defendant John David Stutts and unknown codefendants in handling of a firearm. The plaintiff asks the court for compensatory and punitive damages against the defendants.

The new form communicated everything necessary in 37 words. The old form still had not explained the underlying allegation despite wasting 54 words so far.
See also **style guides**.

legislature

Capitalize when preceded by the name of a state or a specific number: the Utah Legislature, the 44th Legislature. Keep capitalization when the state name is dropped but the reference is specifically to that state's legislature.

less, fewer

see **fewer, less.**

licorice

Spelled thus. Not *liquorice*, the British spelling. Commonly misspelled with an *h*.

lists

You may leave a list of three or fewer items within the text of the paragraph, but do not individually label each item. Lists of more than three items should appear in a *displayed list*: that is, broken into a numbered or bulleted listing that is indented one level deeper than the originating text. Each item in a displayed list must be labeled.

In a displayed list, capitalize the first word of each item.

When a list is used in the imperative mood or continues an introductory sentence, use semicolons (when one or more of the items in the list contains an internal comma) or commas (when none of the items in the list contains an internal comma) after all but the last item and use a period after the last item.

When using a list of items that complete the introductory sentence, make sure each item is parallel in structure. See **parallel structure**.

When each item in a list is a complete thought by itself, end each item with a period.
See **commas** and **semi-colons**.

longstanding

Spelled thus and no longer hyphenated even when used as an adjective.

long-term

Hyphenated. Lowercase *-term*: Long-term parking.

lose, loose

Not synonymous, and another pair of words that, when misused, are a shining beacon indicating that the document's writer is unprofessional. To *lose* means to fail to win, to misplace, or to cease to be in possession.

Right: Once the star quarterback was injured, the home team knew it would lose the game.

Right: I keep my keys on a peg by the door so I do not lose them.

Loose means the opposite of tight or (less commonly) the opposite of tighten.

Right: The girl's loose tooth finally popped out, so she put it under her pillow for the tooth fairy.

Right: She loosed the hound from its chain so it could run around and explore the yard.

Even though *lose* is pronounced as though it had a double vowel, do not spell *lose* with an extra o:

Wrong: They always loose when they miss so many shots.

Wrong: You'll loose your mind if you keep watching those romantic comedies.

M

makeup (n., adj.)

Spelled thus and not hyphenated when used as a noun or adjective:

The applicant wore tasteful makeup to the job interview.

The student arrived at the Science Building the next morning for her makeup examination.

Separate words when used as a verb phrase:

Storytellers make up whimsical characters and events.

manageable

Don't omit the *e*.

manmade

Despite gender-specific terminology, still the most common usage. Spelled thus and rarely hyphenated. Consider other terms when possible to avoid gender misuse:

Acceptable: The manmade lake. A manmade building. This manmade barrier.

Better: The artificial lake. A prefabricated building. This constructed barrier.

manpower

See also **gender-specific terminology**.

mantel, mantle

A *mantel* is a shelf. A *mantle* is a cloak. Mickey Mantle played center field and first base for the New York Yankees from 1951 to 1968.

markup

See also **makeup**.

may, shall, must

See **inappropriate words** and **active voice**.

microcomputer

Rarely used anymore. *Computer* is acceptable. In some contexts you can use *PC*, but that usage is becoming dated as portable and notebook computers become cheaper and more ubiquitous.

millennium

Two *l*s and two *n*s. Most misspellings omit an *l* or an *n*.

misdemeanor

Spelled thus. Avoid using *misdemeanor* and *felony* unless your writing requires the distinction. The words *crime*, *violation*, and *illegal* are perfectly clear and understandable.

months

When a phrase lists only a month and a year, do not separate the month and year with a comma.

The license expires in January 2009.

See **dates**.

more than, over

Over generally refers to a spatial relationship:

The laser lights were suspended over the stage.
The balcony stood over the rearmost 20 rows of seats.

Over can be used with numbers:

She is over 21.
I paid over $500 for this guitar.

But *more than* may be better:

My paycheck went up more than $100 a month.

Consider how the phrase sounds when read and choose accordingly.

multidimensional
multifamily
multistate
multiyear

The prefix *multi-* is rarely hyphenated anymore. Its meaning is *encompassing more than one of* the entity identified in the suffix, but for identifications of two or three of the suffix entity, consider the prefixes *bi-* and *tri-* instead. *Multi-*, in casual reading, is taken to mean more than a small number of the suffix entity.

must, shall, may

See **inappropriate words** and **active voice**.

mustache

Spelled thus. *Moustache* is the British spelling.

James LaBrie and Mike Portnoy are the two band members who most commonly wear mustaches.

N

nationwide

They're on your side.

nighttime

Dwight's bed-and-breakfast offered guests their choice of the America Room, the Irrigation Room, and the Nighttime Room.

nonappropriated
nonattainment
noncancelable
noncontact
nongovernmental
nonmember
nonprescription
nonprofit
nonsupport
nonvoting

Spelled thus and not hyphenated. Consider phrasing that does not require a *non-* prefixed word:

Acceptable: Is the hospital in a rural area or a nonrural area?
Better: Is the hospital in a rural area or not in a rural area?

Sometimes a rephrase is no improvement. Let your ear be your guide:

Acceptable: Is the new facility a for-profit or nonprofit location?
Better?: Is the new facility a for-profit or not-for-profit location?

Sometimes there is no feasible way to rephrase:

Acceptable: The two advisory members hold nonvoting seats on the Board.
Wrong: The two advisory members hold seats on the Board that are not for voting.

none

It usually means *no single one* and takes a singular verb and pronoun:

None of the guitars was in tune after the marathon performance was over.

Use a plural verb only if the sense is *no two* or *no amount*:

None of the band members were ready to head back into the studio until after a recuperative hiatus.

None of the fans were expecting a concept album so soon after Jordan Rudess joined the band in 1999.

numbers

Spell out whole numbers below 10. Exceptions to this style include numbers in tabular material, equations, and measurements.

Do not use both the number spelled out and its Arabic number equivalent in parentheses.

Avoid beginning a sentence with a number.

For expressions of time, use the abbreviations *a.m.* and *p.m.* in lower case. See **time**.

When using numbers that are 1 million or greater, use a combination of figures and words: The amount of insurance shall be $8 million.

Use a comma to separate groups of three digits: 109,278,345. The exception to this rule is for numbers of four figures: 1000. In this instance, you may omit the comma, but be consistent throughout your document. The increasingly prevalent usage is to always add the comma.
See **fractions** and **ordinals**.

occur, occurred, occurring

The *r* is doubled for the present- and past-tense forms.

office

Capitalize when part of an agency's formal name: on file with the Office of the Secretary of State.
The Office is an NBC television comedy adapted from the British hit show of the same name.

off of

The *of* is unnecessary. The album fell off the charts. Not: The album fell off of the charts.

offhand
offset
offsite
offtrack

Spelled thus and not hyphenated. Generally used informally or as jargon; be careful that your usage is clear, concise, and understandable.

on

Do not use *on* before a date or day of the week when its absence would not lead to confusion:

The concert will be held Friday.
The album is due out October 6, 2009.

Use *on* to avoid any suggestion that a date is the object of a transitive verb:

The band canceled on Monday their upcoming radio appearance so that James could recover from a head cold.

The Senate killed on March 9th the telecommunications tax surcharge bill.

one-

Hyphenate when used in writing fractions: one-half, one-fourth.
See **fractions**.

one-sided

Spelled thus and hyphenated. Best used to denote lack of objectivity:

Police reports are one-sided documents used to aid in the prosecution of crimes, not impartial accounts of events regarding an arrest and charge against a defendant.

online

One word in all cases for the computer connection term. Never hyphenated anymore.

onsite

Onsite is not hyphenated as an adjective or adverb.

ordinals

Spell out ordinals below *10th* except if it would detract from readability (such as in a Table): The second album, third-party equipment.
See **numbers** and **fractions**.

outreach

Use instead of *field* in social services contexts: Outreach clinics, outreach visits.

The adjective *field* fell into disuse when researchers determined that people thought a *field clinic* was a clinic held in a field, grassy meadow and all.

over, more than

See **more than, over**.

overall

A single word when not describing a spatial or qualitative relationship.

Overall, Dream Theater's career improved markedly when they added James LaBrie as frontman.

James LaBrie was chosen over all other vocalists who sent sample recordings.

The overall policy is to err on the side of safety.

P

palate, palette, pallet

Palate is the roof of the mouth. A *palette* is an artist's paint board or the electronic representation of the same. A *pallet* is a bed or small platform.

parallel, paralleled, paralleling

Spelled thus. Avoid doubling the second *l*.

parallel structure

Arrange items in a list so that parallel ideas have parallel construction.

NONPARALLEL (Wrong):

The band manager's duties are:
1. To arrange for the band's lodging, (phrase)
2. The band manager signs all contracts, and (clause)
3. Issuing of all paychecks and bonuses. (topic)

PARALLEL CONSTRUCTION (Right):

The duties of the band manager are to:
1. Arrange for the band's lodging,
2. Sign all contracts, and
3. Issue all paychecks and bonuses.

parentheses

When possible, avoid using parentheses unless it is absolutely the simplest, clearest, cleanest way to convey the meaning in your text. Use semicolons or dashes instead.

Wrong: John Myung plays six-stringed basses. (They are the type he prefers.)
Right: John Myung plays six-stringed basses; they are the type he prefers.
Right: John Myung plays six-stringed basses -- they are the type he prefers.
Right: John Myung plays six-stringed basses (guitars).

See also **dash, semi-colon.**

part time, part-time

Hyphenate when used as a compound modifier:

He works part time. He has a part-time job.

passthrough

Spelled thus and not hyphenated.

percent

Style guides differ, but the prevailing usage is toward the symbol % and no longer having the word *percent* spelled out. As long as you are consistent within your document and you are not directed to use one style or the other, choose according to what looks and reads cleanest. A document that is fairly light on figures and statistics might read better with *percent*, while a document containing data, especially with tables, should almost certainly use % instead.

Percent or % takes a singular verb when standing alone or when a singular word follows an of construction:

The venue manager said 95% is the typical ticket sell-through before the day of the show.
The report said 30% of the population agrees.

It takes a plural verb when a plural word follows an of construction:

The faculty said 75% of the students were finished with the test in less than an hour.

Repeat % with each individual figure:

The dean's office said 40% to 45% of the students finished the semester with at least a B average.

permissible

Spelled thus. *Permissable* sounds correct, but is not.

persuade, convince

See **convince, persuade**.

phenomenon, phenomena

Never *phenomenons*.

plurals

Do not make a noun or a verb plural by adding the plural form in parentheses. Use either the singular form or the plural form. In general, the singular form is the default and should be used any time you do not explicitly mean a plural quantity.

Wrong: graph(s), ability(ies), or word(s)
Right: graph, ability, or word
Right: graphs, abilities, or words
Right: graph or graphs, ability or abilities, word or words

See **singular form**.

p.m., a.m.

See **time**.

policyholder

Spelled thus and not hyphenated.

positive writing

Negative sentences can be difficult to understand.

Wrong: No application shall be accepted unless it is signed by the submitter.
Wrong: The application shall not be signed by a person who is not the submitter.
Right: The submitter shall sign the application.

A negative statement can be clear. Use it if you are cautioning the reader: No smoking.

Avoid several negatives in one sentence.

Wrong: A position may not be offered if all application requirements are not met.
Right: A position shall be offered only if the applicant meets all requirements.

possessives

Avoid using of phrases (grades of students) when an apostrophe and s construction is possible:

driver's license, drivers' licenses, attorney's license, parent's responsibility, plaintiff's burden of proof.

Certain phrases indicating the passage of time are possessives: a day's pay, five years' experience.

postaudit
postclosure
postgraduate
postsecondary

Not hyphenated. The prefix *post-* always means *subsequent to* the event or condition identified in the suffix. Usually used as an adjective, but: *postmortem* (noun); *postmortem examination* (adjective).

powerhouse

Spelled thus and not hyphenated. If you are writing a document having anything to do with sports, avoid this term no matter how well the winning team or school performed. It is among the most overused sports clichés.

praiseworthy

Spelled thus and not hyphenated.

preaudit
preconstruction
preempt
preexist

Not hyphenated. The prefix *pre-* always means *prior to* the event or condition identified in the suffix. Usually used as an adjective, but: *predate* (verb); *preempt* (verb); *preemptive strike* (noun).

present tense

An instruction of continuing effect speaks of the time it is applied, not of the time it is written or when it becomes effective.

Wrong: The fine for damage to the hotel bathroom shall be $100.
Right: The fine for damage to the hotel bathroom is $100.

Wrong: When it has been determined by the band that the recording that was completed in the studio is acceptable...
Right: When the band determines that the studio recording is acceptable...

principal, principle

Principal means main or chief, or the sum of money on which interest accrues. *Principle* means moral standard or belief.

I paid extra toward the principal because, on general principle, I do not wish to carry excessive amounts of debt.

printout

Spelled thus as a noun. Separate words when used as a verb.

pursuant to

Avoid using *pursuant to*. Use *according to*, *under*, *following*, or *by*. *Pursuant to* is archaic legalese.

Q

questionnaire

Consider using *survey* instead.

quotation marks

As the Associated Press Stylebook states, follow these long-established printers' rules:

The period and the comma always go within the quotation marks.

The dash, the semicolon, the question mark, and the exclamation point go within the quotation marks when they apply to the quoted matter only. They go outside when they apply to the whole sentence.

R

retroactive

Preferable to the Latin term *ex post facto*.

recordkeeping

Recordkeeping is not hyphenated, either as a noun or adjective.

recur, recurred, recurring

An event or instance can only be called a *recurrence* when it is substantially the same event or instance that came before. If enough aspects of the event or instance have changed, it did not recur, but instead was a separate *occurrence*.

reign, rein

Not synonymous. A *reign* is the duration of a ruler's authority. A *rein* is a device used to control the movements of an animal, usually a horse.

To *take the reins* means to assume control. *Free rein* means the absence of restraints.

The parliament gave the popular king free rein of authority for the duration of his reign.

relabeling

See **editing and relabeling**.

rescission

The result of something being rescinded. Used in formal communication.

restroom

Not *bathroom, toilet, water closet, men's room, ladies' room,* or *thinkin' throne.*

runoff

Spelled thus as both noun and adjective and not hyphenated.

Neither candidate earned 50% of the vote, so there will be a runoff election.

The city dug a channel near the landfill to route the storm runoff out of nearby neighborhoods to the waste reservoir.

S

scientific names

See **italics**.

seasons

Lowercase *spring*, *summer*, *fall*, *autumn*, *winter*, and derivatives such as *springtime* unless part of a formal name:

Metallica's *Summer Sanitarium* Tour.
Trans-Siberian Orchestra's holiday song *Wizards in Winter*.

second-hand (adj.)

Spelled thus and hyphenated. The hyphen may never disappear because the two-word version of the phrase means a part of a clock (*second hand*) while the hyphenated phrase means *previously owned*.

semiannual
semiautomatic
semifinal
semimonthly

Unlike *pre-*, *post-*, *multi-*, and similar prefixes, *semi-* has variations in meaning based on the nature of the suffix term. A *semiannual party* occurs twice per year. A *semiautomatic weapon* fires once for each press of the trigger instead of firing continuously, but does not need to be reset before it can fire again. A *semifinal* is the contest that occurs before the final contest. Be certain of the definition of the word you are using if it has the *semi-* prefix.

semi-colons

Use a semi-colon when two independent clauses are related and emphasis is placed equally on both clauses.

Use a semi-colon at the end of each list item or subsection that completes the thought of the list opening phrase or previous level of subsection if none of the items in the list is a complete sentence and if at least one of the items in the list contains a comma. If no item in the list contains a comma, use commas at the end of each item.

See **commas** and **lists**.

serviceable

Spelled thus. A common misspelling omits the second *e*.

set up (v.), setup (n., adj.)

See **makeup**.

sewage, sewerage

Sewage is waste matter. *Sewerage* is the draining system.

shall, must may

See **inappropriate words** and **active voice**.

sizable

Spelled thus. A common misspelling adds an unnecessary *e* after the *z*.

skeptic, skeptical

Spelled thus. *Sceptic* and *sceptical* are British spellings.

soundproof

Not *soundproofed*.

Dream Theater records album tracks in a soundproof room at the studio.

spacing

The use of two spaces after a colon, period, or state abbreviation has fallen into disuse. It was necessary for kerning purposes when most publishing took place via the printing press. Most common word-processing software suites automatically kern and align text, obviating the need for the additional space. Writers who were taught to type using the two-space style often continue to use it. Whether you choose to place one space or two spaces after colons, periods, and state abbreviations, make sure you are consistent throughout your document.

spelling

Do not depend on spelling checkers in software! Spelling checkers are not accurate for many proper nouns, scientific terms, Latin terms, and other words. A classic error that tells a hiring manager the applicant did not proofread his application is seeing *form* where *from* should appear, and vice versa. Both are common English words, so spelling checkers do not indicate an error.

Wrong: I worked as a sales representative at Roadrunner Records form July 2002 to March 2004.
Wrong: Please find enclosed my completed application from. Thank you for your consideration.

standby

Spelled thus and not hyphenated when a noun or adjective. Two separate words when used as a verb.

staples

If possible, find out if your recipient expects a stapled document. Sometimes an office must scan all documents for archiving, making staples a hindrance. In other cases, a professor may simply want a paper clip she can easily remove while grading a dissertation.
Staples is a chain of retail stores specializing in office supplies.

state

Lowercase in all state of constructions: the state of Nevada, licensees in this state.

Capitalize when it is part of an agency title: State Board of Nursing.

statewide

Spelled thus and not hyphenated.

stationary, stationery

To stand still is to be *stationary*. Writing paper is *stationery*.

stockholder

Spelled thus and not hyphenated. Used as a noun or adjective:

All stockholders are invited to the company's annual stockholder conference.

style guides

The appropriate style guide for a given document varies by the document's type and formality.

In general, *The Chicago Manual of Style*, published by the University of Chicago Press, is safe to follow for general applications. If you are a career climber and you are not in the legal, medical, or academic fields, it is unlikely that you will be directed to use any other style guide.

For academic documents not scientific in nature, the prevalent usage is the Modern Language Association of America's *MLA Style Manual and Guide to Scholarly Publishing*. For academic documents that are scientific, use instead the American Psychological Association (APA) Style as published in the *APA Publication Manual*. Consult your university's academic guidelines before submitting any critical documents.

For legal writing, unless your jurisdiction specifies otherwise, use *The Bluebook: A Uniform System of Citation*, compiled by the Harvard Law Review, Columbia Law Review, University of Pennsylvania Law Review, and Yale Law Journal. Some jurisdictions may allow, prefer, or even require instead the *ALWD Citation Manual*, compiled by the Association of Legal Writing

Directors. For example, the U.S. Court of Appeals for the 11th Circuit requires documents to be formatted according to the *ALWD Citation Manual*.

subcommittee
subcontract
subcutaneous
subduction
submarine
subordinate
subterranean

Not hyphenated. The prefix *sub-* always means *underneath* or *under the purview of* the entity identified in the suffix. Used in adjective, noun, and verb forms:

The architect knew he would have to subcontract the masonry to an outside vendor.

There are ten times as many submarine species as land-based species.

Earthquakes are caused by the tectonic process of subduction.

Also:
The supervisor had four subordinates.

The supervisor subordinated the September project to the completion of more pressing matters.

suspensive hyphenation

The form: The 8- and 9-year-olds attend afternoon classes.

symbols

Be careful when using symbols. Not all symbols translate across different fonts, and not all symbols remain after your text is copied-and-pasted to different software.
See also **fractions**.

T

telephone numbers

The form: (800) 555-1212.
If there is an extension, (800) 555-1212, ext. 789 (abbreviated and lowercase *ext.*).
The parentheses around the area code are based on a format that telephone companies have agreed upon for domestic and international communications.

temperature

See **Celsius** and **Fahrenheit**.

that (conjunction)

Use the conjunction *that* to introduce a dependent clause if the sentence sounds or looks awkward without it. *That* is often unnecessary, but in general:

That should be used when a time element intervenes between the verb and the dependent clause: The president said Monday that he had signed the bill.

That usually is necessary after some verbs. They include: *advocate, assert, contend, declare, estimate, make clear, point out, propose,* and *state.*

That is required before subordinate clauses beginning with conjunctions such as *after, although, because, before, in addition to, until*, and *while*:

The band manager declared that after the next two shows, the road crew would be given a day off.

that, which

The distinction between *that* and *which* is so frequently misapplied that it has become one of the clarion signals indicating whether a document was written professionally. Learning correct usage of *that* and *which* is almost as important as learning correct apostrophe usage.

Use *who* and *whom* for references to people. Use *that* and *which* for inanimate objects and animals:

Jordan Rudess is the musician who most recently joined the band.

He has a special keyboard that can be played by sliding a finger across a touchpad.

That sets off a restrictive or essential clause and is used without commas:

The Amazon is the river that gives Brazil life. (restrictive)

Which sets off a non-restrictive or non-essential clause and is used with commas:

The Amazon, which flows into the Atlantic Ocean, gives Brazil life. (non-restrictive)

If you have been using *that* and *which* incorrectly, do not be discouraged. This mistake is common even in famous written and creative works. In *The Phantom of the Opera*, Andrew Lloyd Webber errs by having the Phantom, who has captured Christine, ask Raoul, "Why would I make her bleed / For the sins which are yours?" A more correct grammatical construction would have been "For the sins *that* are yours," and the rhyming scheme would not have been disrupted by the correction. (The most correct phrasing of all would have been "For your sins," but that would not have fit into the rhyming scheme.) If Webber can make such a mistake, it is no shame for the rest of us to do the same. Consider, then, how much it improves your document when you use *that* and *which* correctly!

theater, theatre

Typically *theater* is the American usage and *theatre* is British. Proper nouns should remain spelled as they are regardless of other usage: Dream Theater; the Springfield Community Theatre Group.

Dream Theater was named after a California art-house movie venue after the band learned that their original moniker, Majesty, was already held under another trademark.

third-party (adj.), third party (n.)

Hyphenate when used as an adjective.
Always lowercase -*party*.

time

Lowercase *a.m.* and *p.m.*, and use periods and minute numbers. 2:00 p.m., not 2 PM.
Avoid the use of *noon* and *midnight* if possible. Industries that operate on a 24-hour basis have adopted methods of avoiding confusion. For example, transportation and mass media companies schedule flights or broadcasts for 12:01 a.m. or 11:59 p.m. This makes it obvious what time the scheduled event will occur. It also avoids confusion such as with the phrase *the meeting will occur about Saturday midnight* -- does that mean at the beginning of

Saturday, just after Friday night, or at the end of Saturday, just before Sunday morning? The use of a 24-hour clock, common in Europe, is still rarely seen in the U.S. except in military and medical applications. Style guides differ whether midnight is 00:00 or 24:00 on the 24-hour clock, though 00:00 has become the prevailing form in recent years.

time-frame

Time-frame is hyphenated when used as a noun or adjective. Lowercase *-frame* in all uses.

total, totaled, totaling

Do not duplicate the *l*.

toward

Not *towards*.

transfer, transferred, transferring

Spelled thus, duplicating the *r* as appropriate.

travel, traveled, traveling

Do not duplicate the *l*.

U

under, below

Avoid using prepositions that indicate direction or location when indicating quantity.
See **more than, over**.

unique

It means one of a kind. Avoid describing something as *rather unique* or *fairly unique*. That is an error similar to describing someone as *rather pregnant* or *fairly pregnant*.

unnecessary words

If it is possible to omit a word and preserve the desired meaning, always omit the word.

Acceptable: I will go to work on Friday.
Better: I will work Friday.

Omit language that is meaningless or confusing.

Wrong: The Department shall maximize its deficit reduction program and enforce a positive downsizing in the personnel pool.
Right: The Department shall cut costs and lay off employees.

upward

Not *upwards*.

U.S.

U.S. in all uses when abbreviating *United States*, not *US*. Do not use *U.S.* as a noun.

V

v. or vs.

Do not italicize in the formal title of a legal case:

Kelo v. *New London* (2005) is one of the worst Supreme Court decisions in the history of jurisprudence.

vacuum

A common misspelling adds an extra *c*.

verb tense and voice

See **present tense** and **active voice**.

vice versa

Hyphenation varies but is becoming less common.

videotape

Obsolete. Consider using *video recording* (noun) or *record* (verb) or other technologically neutral term unless you are referring to an actual videocassette.

W

wastewater
waterborne
waterproof

Spelled thus and not hyphenated.

web site

Usage is still new. Compounding into *website* is becoming increasingly common.

which, that

See **that, which**.

who, whom

Use *who* and *whom* for references to people. Use *that* and *which* for inanimate objects and animals:

Chris Collins was the vocalist who sang with Dream Theater in their first public performance.

Spot was the dog that we found wandering around by the river.

Use *who* when someone is the subject of a sentence, clause, or phrase:

The entrant who submits the best fan video will win the autographed guitar.

Use *whom* when someone is the object of a verb or preposition:

The band shall determine to whom the autographed guitar will be awarded.

The simple rule of thumb is to use *whom* when *him* would sound correct and to use *who* when *he* would sound correct. Let your ear be your guide.

wildlife

The World Wildlife Fund won exclusive use of the acronym WWF, forcing the World Wrestling Federation to change its name to World Wrestling Entertainment, or WWE. Despite the change in the organization's name, the fights the WWE stages remain as real as three-dollar bills.

workers' compensation

Always a plural possessive. Never *worker's compensation*.

workload
workspace
wrongdoing

Never used with a hyphen anymore.

XYZ

years

Years are the lone exception to the general rule in numerals that a figure is not used to start a sentence: 2008 marked the Cardinals' first NFC West title in 33 years.

Use Arabic figures to indicate decades of history. Add the letter *s* and no apostrophe to show the plural: the 1970s, the mid-1990s.

Use an apostrophe to indicate missing numerals: the roaring '20s; the nifty '50s. *But*: San Francisco 49ers, Philadelphia 76ers.

ZIP code

Put one space between the state abbreviation and the ZIP code: Beverly Hills, CA 90210. New York, NY 10001.

Bibliography

Arizona Rulemaking Manual. Office of the Secretary of State of Arizona. Phoenix, Arizona, 2003.

Block, Gertrude, Effective Legal Writing, Second Edition. The Foundation Press, Inc., Mineola, New York, 1983.

Freeman, Lawrence H., Ph.D. and Terry R. Bacon, Ph.D., Style Guide: Revised Edition. Shipley Associates, Bountiful, Utah, 1990.

Goldfarb, Ronald L. and James C. Raymond, Clear Understandings. Random House, New York, New York, 1982.

Goldstein, Norm, Ed., Associated Press Stylebook and Briefing on Media Law. Perseus Publishing, Cambridge, Massachusetts, 2000.

Office of the Federal Register, "Rule Writing - A Practical Approach." March, 1985. (Approved by the Arizona Governor's Regulatory Review Council, and printed by the Arizona Executive Budget Office, 1990.)

Redish, Janice C., Ph.D., "How to Write Regulations And Other Legal Documents In Clear English." American Institutes for Research, Washington, D.C., 1991.

Rosen, Leonard J., The Everyday English Handbook. Doubleday & Co., Garden City, New York, 1985.

Sabin, William A., The Gregg Reference Manual. Macmillan/McGraw Hill Publishing Company, New York, New York.

State Bar of Arizona, Administrative Law Section, Rosie Rule. Phoenix, Arizona, December 1999.

Strunk, William Jr. and E.B. White, The Elements of Style. Macmillan Publishing Co., New York, New York, 1979.

Thompson, Margaret H. and J. Harold Janis, Revised Standard Reference for Secretaries and Administrators. Macmillan Publishing Co., New York, New York, 1980.

University of Chicago Press, The Chicago Manual of Style -- 14th Ed. Chicago, IL 1993.

Venolia, Jan, Rewrite Right!: How to Revise Your Way to Better Writing. Ten Speed Press/Periwinkle Press, Berkeley, California, 1987.

Weihofen, Henry, Legal Writing Style, Second Edition. West Publishing Co., St. Paul, Minnesota, 1980.

Wydick, R.C., Plain English for Lawyers. Academic Press, Durham, N.C., 1979.

NOTES

NOTES

www.ingramcontent.com/pod-product-compliance
Lightning Source LLC
Chambersburg PA
CBHW060337290526
45793CB00003B/644